All for STRINGS

COMPREHENSIVE STRING METHOD ■ BOOK 2
by Gerald E. Anderson and Robert S. Frost

Dear String Student:

Welcome to **ALL FOR STRINGS, Book 2!**

By now, you have discovered that careful study and regular practice have brought you the joy and satisfaction of playing beautiful music.

The new playing technics and musical concepts found in **ALL FOR STRINGS, Book 2,** will help you to continue your progress as a string player and musician.

We hope that **ALL FOR STRINGS, Book 2,** will help make the road to your musical goals more enjoyable.

Best wishes!

Gerald E. Anderson
Robert S. Frost

ALL FOR STRINGS, Book 2, is published for the following instruments:
   Violin   Viola   Cello   String Bass

Piano Accompaniment
   A separate book containing 82 piano accompaniments is recommended to students for home use, private instruction and ensemble practice.

ISBN 0-8497-3237-9

kjos NEIL A. KJOS MUSIC COMPANY • SAN DIEGO, CALIFORNIA

TUNING

In order for your stringed instrument to sound properly, it is important that each of the strings be tuned to a specific pitch. The pitch of each string should be checked before each playing session. Small changes in pitch are common on a stringed instrument due to the stretching of the string and various changes in temperature and humidity. Strings that are not in tune should be adjusted so that they produce the proper pitch. The procedure outlined on these pages will aid you in making these adjustments.

PRE-TUNING CHECKLIST

Know which type of pegs and strings are on your instrument.

1. Pegs – Conventional: These pegs are held in place by friction. Push the peg inward as you turn to keep it from slipping.
2. Pegs – Patent: These pegs have a tension screw in one end. They are designed to remain in place after turning.
3. Metal strings: Strings with metal loops at the end should be attached to a string adjuster (fine tuner) on the tailpiece. See Figure 2.
4. Metal Wound on Gut Strings: Strings with a knot tied in one end should be attached directly into the tailpiece through the slit provided. See Figure 2.

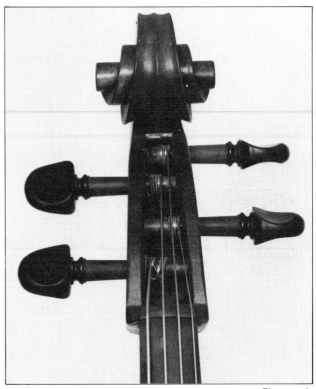

Figure 1

Figure 2

REFERENCE PITCHES

1. A piano, pitch pipe, electronic tuner or another instrument can be used for reference to tune the open strings on the cello.
2. The strings on the cello are five (5) notes apart in pitch. (e.g. D̲ E F G A̲) See Figure 3.
3. The strings are usually tuned in the following sequence: A D G C.
4. Memorize the sound of each reference pitch. Repeat the pitch by humming or singing to get it established in your ear as you tune each string.

Figure 3

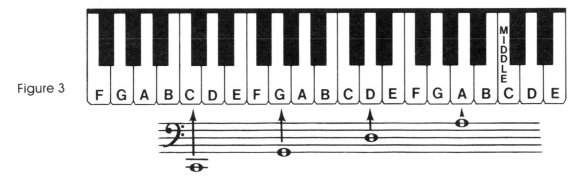

TUNING PROCEDURE

1. Hold the cello in front of you so that you can pluck the string with the thumb of one hand and turn the peg or adjuster with the other hand. See Figures 4 and 5.
2. Sound, listen and memorize the reference pitch. Pluck the correct string. Listen to both sounds and determine if the string sounds higher, lower or the same as the reference pitch.
3. If both the reference pitch and the pitch of the string are the same, go to the next string. If they are different, use the following procedures:
   a. If the string is too high, lower the pitch by turning the peg slightly backward ↓ or the string adjuster counter clockwise. ↻
   b. If the string is too low, raise the pitch by turning the peg slightly forward ↑ or the string adjuster clockwise. ↻
   Continue making adjustments until the string and the reference pitch sound the same.
4. <u>Large adjustments</u> in pitch are made by using the pegs. Turn the peg just a <u>little</u> at a time.
   Caution: If you tune the string <u>too</u> far above its intended pitch you may break the string.
   Reminder: Push the peg into the peg box as you turn it.
5. Small adjustments in pitch are made by turning the string adjusters (fine tuners). See Figure 5.
6. Tune each string in sequence. After you have tuned each string, check all four strings one final time.

Figure 4

Figure 5

BUILDING CORRECT POSITIONS

Building correct positions is a continuous process. The photos, position check and bow grip exercises are to help you with each important element necessary to establish correct positions on your instrument.

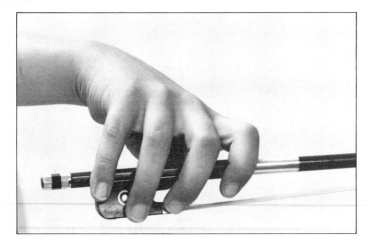

POSITION CHECK

Right Hand
☐ Thumb bent
☐ First finger over the stick
☐ Little finger over the stick

Playing Position
☐ Instrument up
☐ End pin adjusted properly
☐ Sitting up properly

Left Hand
☐ Wrist straight
☐ Elbow up
☐ Thumb behind second finger

Bowing Position
☐ Bow tilted toward fingerboard
☐ Bow pressed into the string
☐ Straight bow stroke

BOW GRIP EXERCISES

Your teacher will explain how to do these exercises.

1. Finger Lifter
2. Flex
3. Wave
4. Teeter-Totter

5. Squeeze-Relax
6. Windshield Wiper No. 1
7. Spider
8. Rocket Launch

9. Bow Lifter
10. Push Up
11. Sidewinder
12. Windshield Wiper No. 2

1. D MAJOR

★ Play lines 1 and 2 with the following bowings:

a.   b.   c.

2. D MAJOR REVIEW

★ Be sure to use a straight bow stroke.

| DÉTACHÉ | 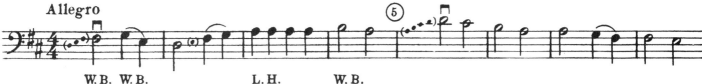 | Détaché bowing is played on the string using separate bows with one note per bow, alternating down bow and up bow. |

NEW IDEA

3. BROTHER JOHN

Round

Moderato

I.   II.

f

III.   IV.

★ Check your bow grip often.

4. SYMPHONY NO. 104-THEME

Haydn

Allegro

W. B. W. B.   L. H.   W. B.

★ Finger preparations are important for good intonation.

5. RHYTHM TEASER

THEORY GAME

★ 1. Write in the counting.   2. Clap and count.   3. Play arco or pizzicato.

6. G MAJOR

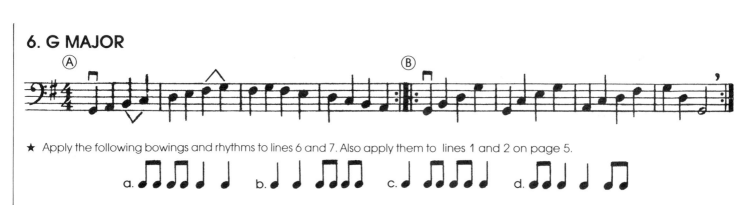

★ Apply the following bowings and rhythms to lines 6 and 7. Also apply them to lines 1 and 2 on page 5.

7. G MAJOR REVIEW

★ Check your left hand position.

8. THERE'S A HOLE IN THE BUCKET

Folk Song

★ Check your instrument position often.

9. RHYTHM TEASER

THEORY GAME

1. Write in the counting.   2. Clap and count.   3. Play arco or pizzicato.

10. RED RIVER VALLEY

American Folk Song

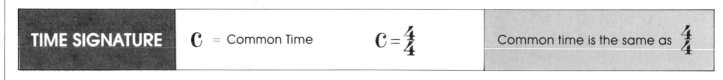

★ Lift and place the bow gently at the bow lifts.

NEW IDEA

| TIME SIGNATURE | **C** = Common Time | **C** = $\frac{4}{4}$ | Common time is the same as $\frac{4}{4}$ |

11. LAME TAME CRANE

Round

12. C MAJOR

★ Apply the following slurred staccato and louré bowings to lines 12 and 13.   Also apply these bowings to review lines 1, 2, 6 and 7.

13. C MAJOR REVIEW

★ Roll the bow to the new string.

14. GOODNIGHT

Round

★ Play with your best tone.

15. ETUDE

Wohlfahrt Op. 38, no.40

★ Use smooth bow changes.

16. BLUE BELLS OF SCOTLAND

Scottish Folk Song

★ Write in the note names.

8

17. SAKURA

Andante

Japanese Folk Song

18. NAME GAME

THEORY GAME

feed   ace   cabbage

★ Draw the notes as indicated in measures 2, 4 and 6.   Name the notes in measures 1, 3, 5, and 7.

19. DUET TIME

Frost-Duet

Allegro

NEW IDEA

LEFT HAND PIZZICATO   A + above a note indicates that a particular note should be played pizzicato with your left hand. Use the fourth (4th) finger of your left hand to pluck the string unless another finger is indicated.

20. LEFT HAND PIZZ.

★ Simile means to continue in the same way.

21. PIZZ. AND ARCO

NEW
NOTES

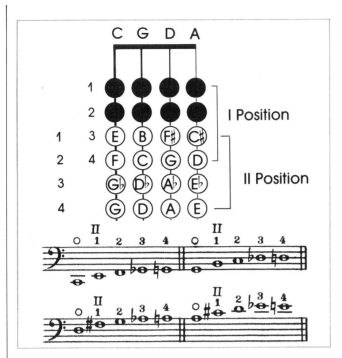

22. SHIFTING TRAINER FOR CELLOS AND BASSES

NEW IDEA

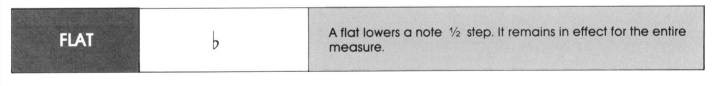

| FLAT | ♭ | A flat lowers a note ½ step. It remains in effect for the entire measure. |

23. NEW NOTES

THEORY
GAME

24. PUMPKIN MUNCHKIN

Anderson

★ What is the form of this selection? _____ form.

NEW
NOTES

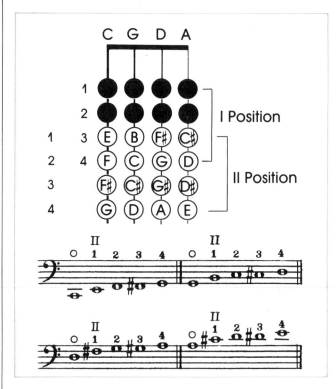

25. SHIFTING TRAINER FOR CELLOS AND BASSES

26. NEW NOTES

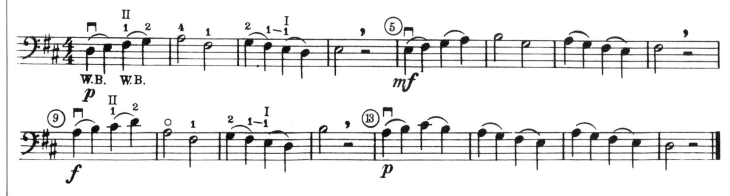

27. MELODY IN D MAJOR

28. TECHNIC TRAINER NO. 1

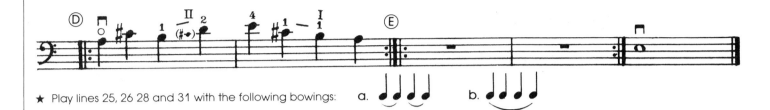

★ Play lines 25, 26 28 and 31 with the following bowings: a.   b.

29. HOLY, HOLY, HOLY!

Dykes

mf

★ Play with your best tone.

30. MUSICAL ADDITION AND SUBTRACTION

★ Write in the type of note or rest that solves each problem.

31. TECHNIC TRAINER NO. 2

32. LIGHTLY ROW   *Memorize

German Folk Song

Moderato

L.H.   W.B.   U.H.   W.B.

★ Use good bow division throughout.

rit.

33. TECHNIC TRAINER NO. 3

34. LITTLE BROWN JUG

Eastburn

Allegro

L.H. W.B. U.H. W.B. L.H.

★ Use good bow division throughout.

35. CARNIVAL OF VENICE

Paganini-Duet

Allegro

36. STRING CROSSING ETUDE

Wohlfahrt Op. 38, no. 46

M.

★ Play line 36 with the following bowing: ♩ ♩ ♩ ♩. Play line 36 with ♫ for each ♩.

37. SMOOTH CROSSINGS

38. SMOOTH SLURS

DOUBLE STOP 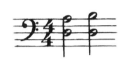 Playing double stops is the technic of playing two strings at the same time.

39. SEVEN STRING LEVELS

40. SMOOTH DOUBLE STOPS

★ Keep even bow pressure on both strings of each double stop.

INTERVAL  G A B C D = 5 letters = interval of a fifth — An interval is the distance between two notes. Counting the number of lines and spaces will tell you the size of the interval.

41. INTERVAL STUDY

★ Determine and write the size of each interval in the blanks provided.

42. SLURRING DOUBLE STOPS

NEW IDEA

EIGHTH REST

$\mathbf{7}$ = ½ beat of silence.

An eighth rest is half as long as a quarter rest.

Counting	1	&	2	&	1	&	2	&
Alternate Counting								

43. RHYTHM TRAINER

★ 1. Clap and count each line.   2. Play arco or pizzicato.   3. Practice each rhythm pattern on the descending scale.

44. RHYTHMIC REUBEN

Duet

★ Also play this line pizzicato.

THEORY GAME

45. MYSTERY SONG

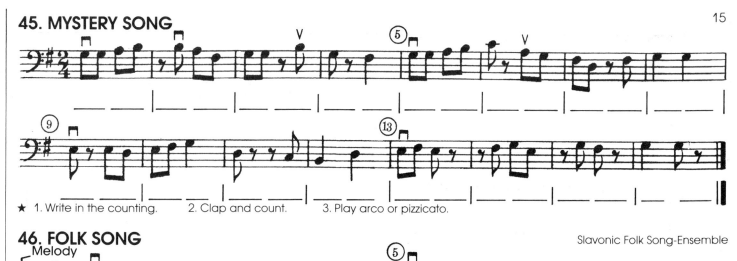

★ 1. Write in the counting.   2. Clap and count.   3. Play arco or pizzicato.

46. FOLK SONG

Slavonic Folk Song-Ensemble

★ Also play line 46 pizzicato.

NEW IDEA

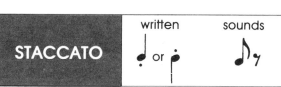

STACCATO

written: ♩ or ♩   sounds: ♪

A dot above or below a note indicates that a note should be played staccato. Staccato is played with separate bows on the string. Separate each note from the next as if a rest were between them.

47. STACCATO TRAINER

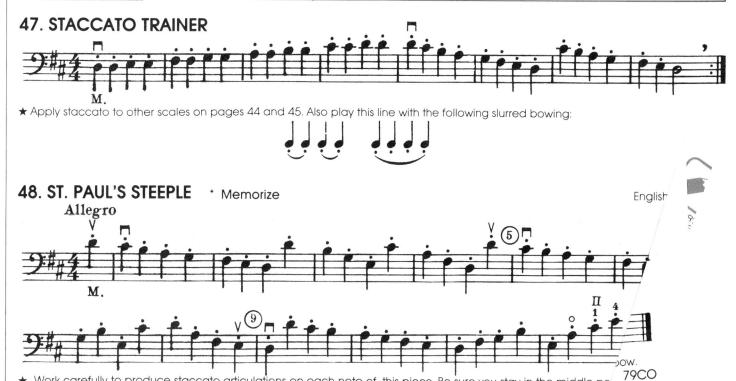

★ Apply staccato to other scales on pages 44 and 45. Also play this line with the following slurred bowing:

48. ST. PAUL'S STEEPLE   * Memorize

Allegro

English

★ Work carefully to produce staccato articulations on each note of this piece. Be sure you stay in the middle po

79CO

DYNAMICS

	= crescendo = *cresc.* = gradually play louder
	= diminuendo = *dim.* = gradually play softer

49. SURPRISE SYMPHONY-THEME
Haydn

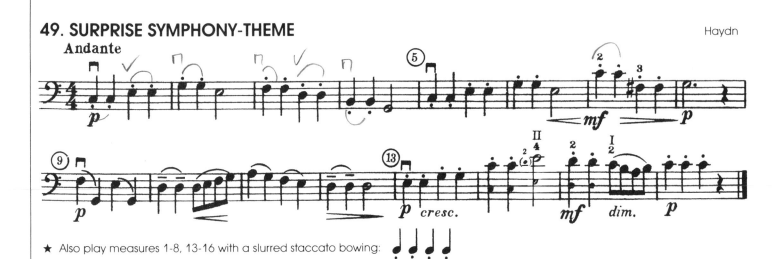

★ Also play measures 1-8, 13-16 with a slurred staccato bowing:

50. ACADEMIC FESTIVAL
Brahms

51. WE WISH YOU A MERRY CHRISTMAS * Memorize
English Carol

52. FIRST SYMPHONY-THEME
Brahms

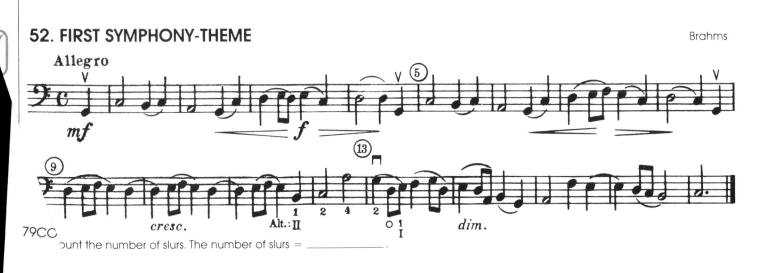

ount the number of slurs. The number of slurs = _____ .

53. TONE DEVELOPER

54. NOW THANK WE ALL OUR GOD

Cruger-Ensemble

★ Play this ensemble at all dynamic levels using your best tone at all times. Remember to keep your bow moving.

55. DOUBLE STOP CHORALE OR MARCH

★ Also use the following rhythm and bowing variations for line 55:

56. RHYTHM TEASER

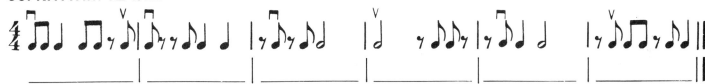

★ 1. Write in the counting.   2. Clap and count.   3. Play arco or pizzicato.

NEW IDEA

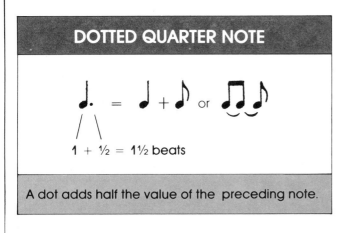

Counting	1 &	2 &	3 &	4 &
Alternate Counting				

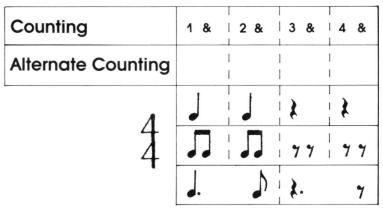

THEORY GAME

57. RHYTHM STUDY

★ 1. Write in the counting.   2. Clap and count.   3. Play arco and pizzicato.

58. AMERICA THE BEAUTIFUL * Memorize

Ward-Ensemble

★ Also play line 58 with the following bowings:

59. SLUR THE RHYTHM

60. ALL THROUGH THE NIGHT   * Memorize

Welsh Folk Song

Andante

★ Check your bow grip often.

61. LITTLE SONG

Mozart

Andante

62. AUGUSTINE

German Folk Song

63. RHYTHM TEASER

★ 1. Write in the counting.   2. Clap and count.   3. Play arco or pizzicato.

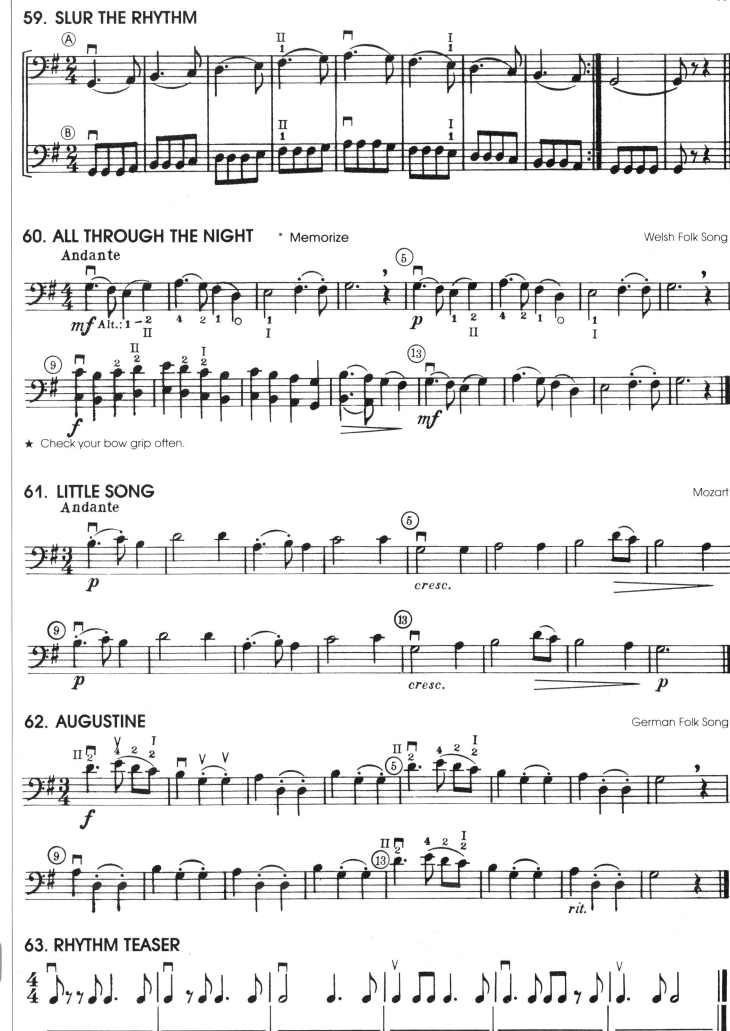

ACCENT

An accent (>) above or below a note indicates that a note should be played with more emphasis. The accent is played by adding a little extra bow pressure with the index finger just before starting the bow stroke.

64. PREPARE THE ACCENT

65. IT'S AN ACCENT

66. MAYPOLE DANCE

67. ACCENT TIME   * Memorize

Frost

68. POSITION CHECK

Right Hand	Playing Position	Left Hand	Bowing Position
☐ Thumb bent	☐ Instrument up	☐ Wrist straight	☐ Bow tilted toward fingerboard
☐ First finger over the stick	☐ End pin adjusted properly	☐ Elbow up	☐ Bow pressed into the string
☐ Little finger over the stick	☐ Sitting up properly	☐ Thumb behind second finger	☐ Straight bow stroke

Have your teacher check your position. Place an X in the box for each item that is correct in your playing.

NEW
NOTES

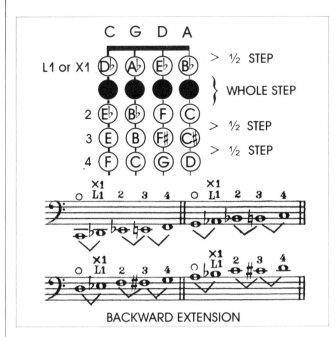

BACKWARD EXTENSION

69. FIRST FINGER TRAINER

70. NEW NOTES

71. TECHNIC TRAINER NO. 4

NEW IDEA

KEY SIGNATURE

This is the key signature for F Major. When you see this key signature, play all the B's as B♭.

72. F MAJOR SCALE AND BROKEN THIRDS

★ Refer to pages 44 and 45 for other bowing and scale possibilities.

78. JUNE LOVELY JUNE

Round

79. SWEET BETSY

Cowboy Song

KEY SIGNATURE		Each major key has a relative minor key. The same key signature is used for both keys. The relative minor scale uses the 6th tone of the major scale for its starting note. There are three forms of the minor scale: natural, harmonic, melodic. This is the key signature for d minor. It is the same as F Major because d minor is the relative minor to F Major.

80. D MINOR SCALES AND ARPEGGIOS

★ Refer to pages 44 and 45 for other bowing and scale possibilities.

81. D MINOR TRAINER

★ Also play line 80 with the following bowing:

82. VOLGA BOATMAN

Russian Folk Song

Andante

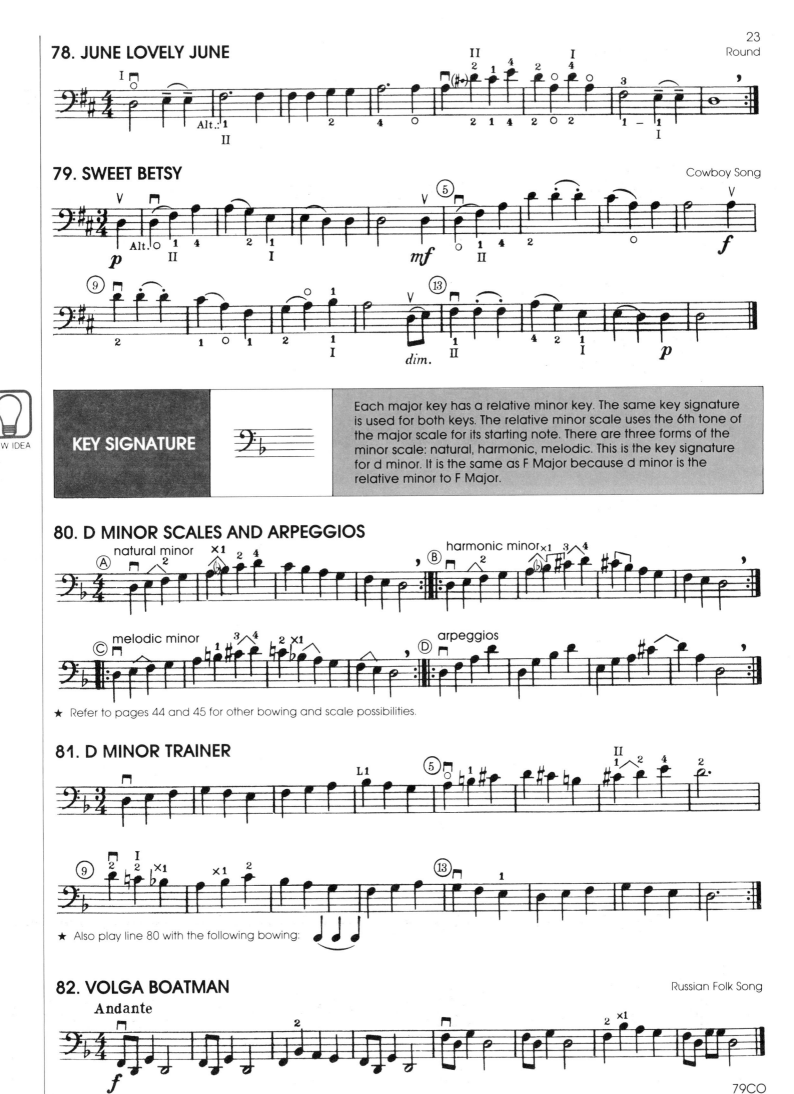

24

83. ERIE CANAL

American Folk Song

★ Check your bow grip often.

84. AMERICA * Memorize

Carey-Ensemble

Moderato

THEORY
GAME

85. DRAW THE NOTES

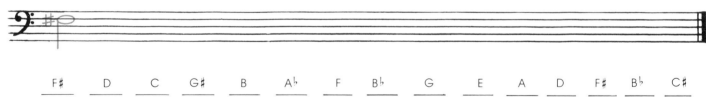

F♯ D C G♯ B A♭ F B♭ G E A D F♯ B♭ C♯

★ Draw a note for each note name listed. Place the accidental on the correct line or space
and to the left of the note head (see example).

86. TECHNIC TRAINER NO. 5

79CO

NEW IDEA

KEY SIGNATURE This is the key signature for B♭ Major. When you see this key signature, play all the B's as B♭ and all the E's as E♭.

87. B♭ MAJOR SCALE AND BROKEN THIRDS

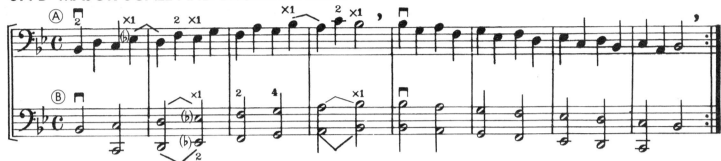

★ Refer to pages 44 and 45 for other bowing and scale possibilities.

88. TECHNIC TRAINER NO. 6

89. ARPEGGIO FUN

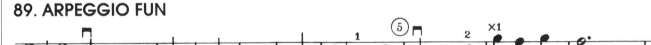

★ Also play this line with the following rhythm:

90. STAR SPANGLED BANNER

Smith

★ Play this anthem with your best tone.

91. RHYTHM TEASER

★ 1. Write in the counting.   2. Clap and count.   3. Play arco or pizzicato.

92. FANCY BLUES

Anderson

NEW IDEA

KEY SIGNATURE   This is the key signature for g minor. It is the same key signature as B♭ Major because g minor is the relative minor key.

93. G MINOR SCALES AND ARPEGGIOS

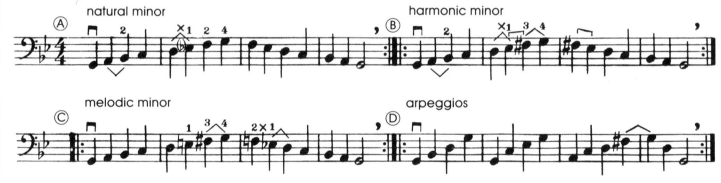

★ Refer to pages 44 and 45 for other bowing and scale possibilities.

94. RUSSIAN MELODY

Russian Folk Song

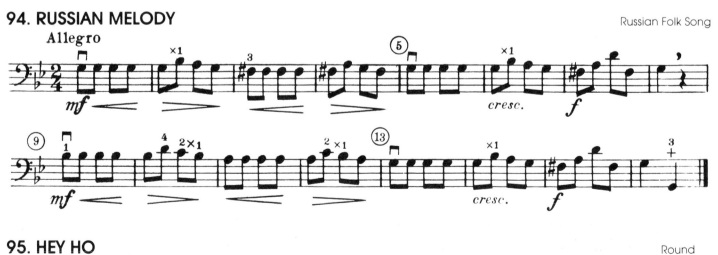

95. HEY HO

Round

96. FINLANDIA-THEME

Sibelius-Ensemble

★ Play this song with your best tone at all dynamic levels.

97. PENCIL PUSHER

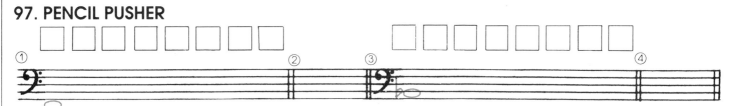

① ③ Draw the notes on the staff to form the F Major and B♭ Major scale. Be sure to include the flats for the appropriate notes. Name each note in the boxes above.

② Draw your clef sign and add the key signature for F Major.

④ Draw your clef sign and add the key signature for B♭ Major.

98. TECHNIC TRAINER NO. 7

NEW IDEA

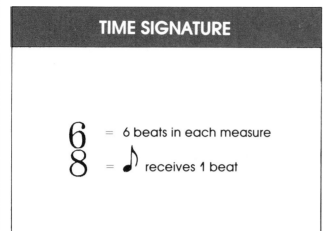

TIME SIGNATURE

$\dfrac{6}{8}$ = 6 beats in each measure

= ♪ receives 1 beat

Counting	1	2	3	4	5	6
Alternate counting						

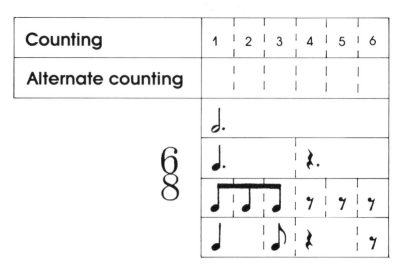

THEORY GAME

99. RHYTHM TRAINER

★ 1. Write in the counting. 2. Clap and count. 3. Play arco or pizzicato.

THEORY GAME

100. OVER THE RIVER

Thanksgiving Song

★ Write in your own dynamics for this song.

THEORY GAME

101. RHYTHM TEASER

★ 1. Write in the counting. 2. Clap and count. 3. Play arco or pizzicato.

102. THANKSGIVING

103. I'D RATHER BE SAILING

Frost-Duet

104. OH DEAR! WHAT CAN THE MATTER BE? * Memorize

English Air

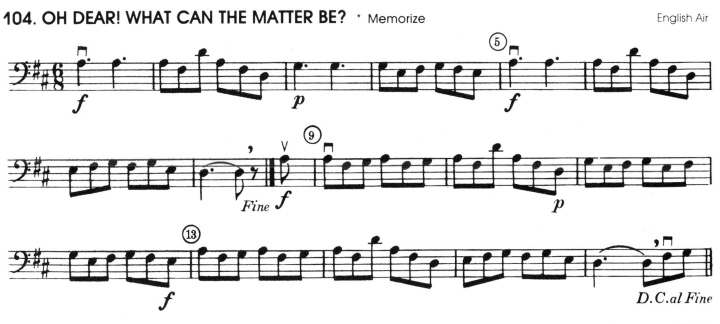

105. FRENCH MARCHING SONG

French Folk Song

106. MUSICAL NOTES AND ROAD SIGNS

L. H. pizz.

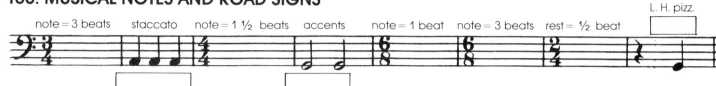

note = 3 beats   staccato   note = 1 ½ beats   accents   note = 1 beat   note = 3 beats   rest = ½ beat

★ Write in the correct musical sign, note or rest value in the measures or boxes provided. Follow the instructions above each measure and be sure to look carefully at each time signature.

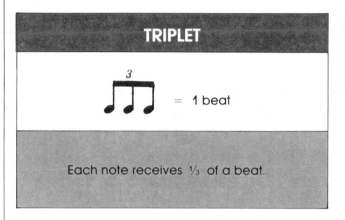

107. RHYTHM TRAINER

★   1. Write in the counting.   2. Clap and count.   3. Play arco or pizzicato.

108. ROW, ROW, ROW YOUR BOAT/LITTLE TOM TINKER

Round-Duet

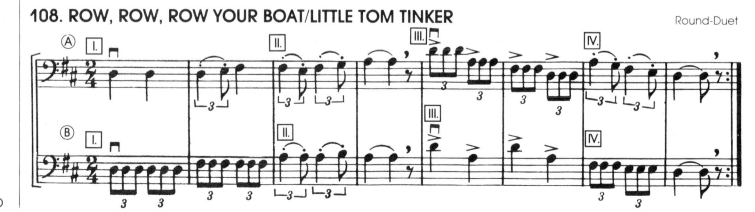

109. TRIPLET TRAINER

★ Also play this line with the following bowing:

110. SYMPHONY NO. 5-THEME

Beethoven

Allegro

111. BEAUTIFUL DREAMER

Foster

★ Do you remember what "D.S. al Fine" means?

112. RHYTHM TEASERS

THEORY
GAME

★ 1. Write in the counting.   2. Clap and count.   3. Play arco or pizzicato.   4. Compare both lines.

32

NEW NOTES

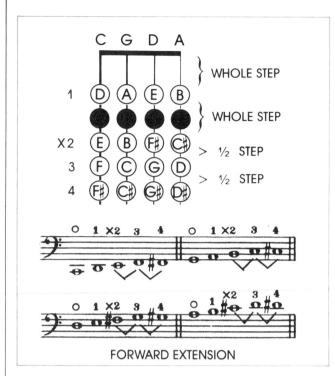

FORWARD EXTENSION

113. NEW NOTES

114. TECHNIC TRAINER NO. 8

NEW IDEA

KEY SIGNATURE — This is the key signature for A Major. When you see this key signature, play all F's as F♯, all C's as C♯ and all G's as G♯.

115. A MAJOR SCALE AND BROKEN THIRDS

★ Refer to pages 44 and 45 for other bowing and scale possibilities.

79CO

116. A MAJOR ETUDE

Wohlfahrt Op. 38, no.82

★ Also play line 116 with the following bowings: a.   b.   c.

117. DU, DU LIEGST MIR IM HERZEN   * Memorize

German Folk Song

Allegro

★ Use smooth bow changes.

118. BELLS OF FREEDOM

Round

119. MARCHING TRIPLETS

Wohlfahrt Op. 38, no. 76

79CO

NEW IDEA

| KEY SIGNATURE | | This is the key signature for a minor. It is the same as C Major because a minor is the relative minor key. |

120. A MINOR SCALES AND ARPEGGIOS

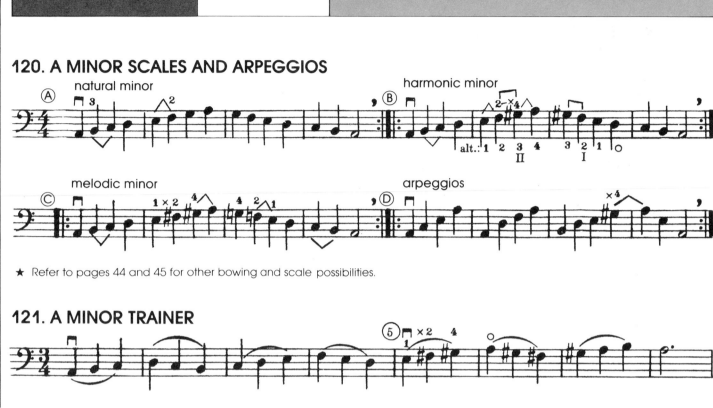

★ Refer to pages 44 and 45 for other bowing and scale possibilities.

121. A MINOR TRAINER

122. TECHNIC TRAINER NO. 9

123. FARANDOLE

Bizet

D. C. al Fine

NEW IDEA

 CHROMATIC

A chromatic scale is built in all half steps. When a piece of music is chromatic, it usually uses notes not normally found in the major or minor key.

124. D CHROMATIC SCALE

125. HABAÑERA

Bizet

Moderato

126. HIGHER OR LOWER

★ Identify the second note in each measure. Below the note write H if it is higher or L if it is lower than the first note.

127. CHROMATIC ETUDE

Wohlfahrt Op. 45, no.16

128. FANTASIA CHROMATICA

Bach

129. O LITTLE TOWN OF BETHLEHEM

Redner

Andante

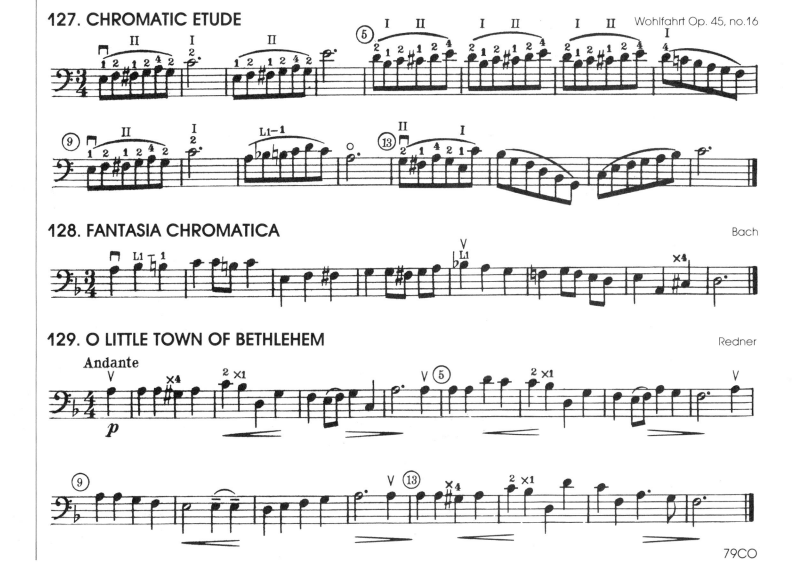

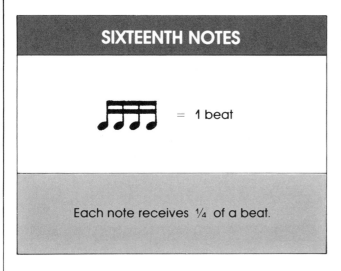

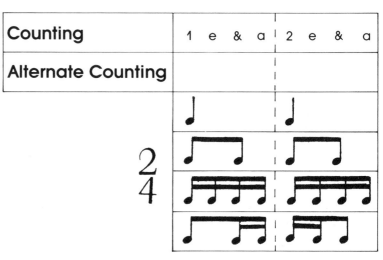

130. RHYTHM TRAINER

★ 1. Write in the counting.   2. Clap and count.   3. Play arco or pizzicato.

131. TIRRA LIRRA LOO

Canadian Folk Song

★ 1. Write in the counting.   2. Clap and count.   3. Play arco or pizzicato.

132. AMERICAN PATROL   * Memorize

Meacham

Allegro

133. WALKING SONG
Moderato

Swiss Folk Song

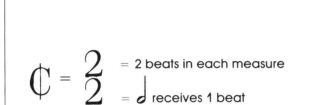

TIME SIGNATURE

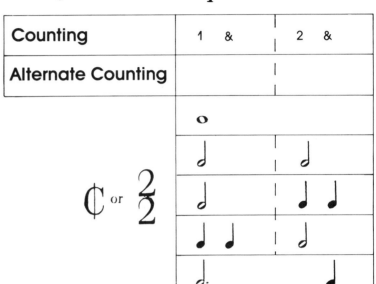

Counting	1	&		2	&
Alternate Counting					

$$\mathbb{C} = \frac{2}{2}$$

= 2 beats in each measure

= 𝅗𝅥 receives 1 beat

𝄵 or $\frac{2}{2}$

THEORY
GAME

134. RHYTHM TRAINER

★ 1. Write in the counting. 2. Clap and count. 3. Play arco or pizzicato.

135. HIGH SCHOOL CADETS
March tempo

Sousa

mp–f

136. STOODLA PUMPA
Andante

Czech Folk Song

mf

p cresc.

f

137. TRICKY YANKEE DOODLE

138. SYMPHONY NO. 40-THEME

Mozart

139. WHEN I WAS A LAD

Sullivan

140. HORNPIPE

Sailors' Dance

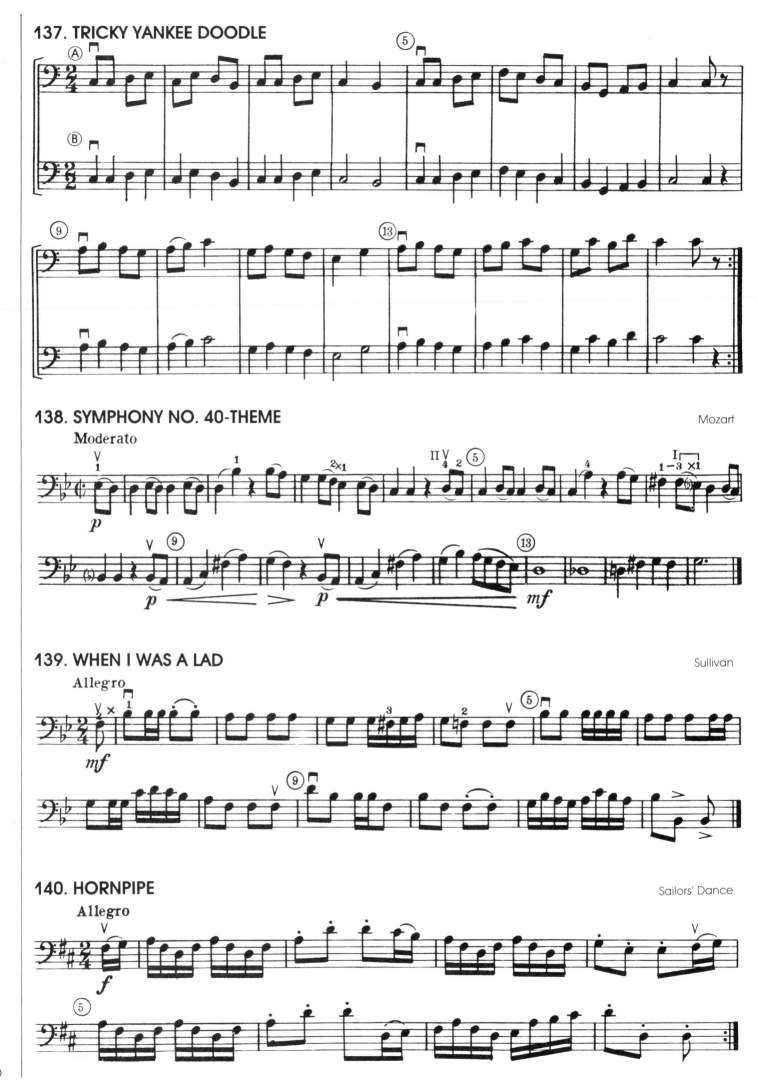

ETUDES

SOLOS

143. THE ASH GROVE

Welsh Folk Song

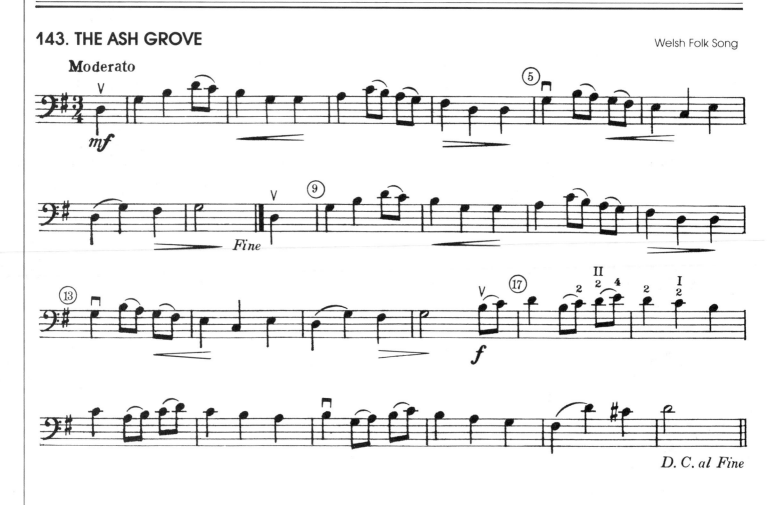

D. C. al Fine

144. MINUET

Bach

2x rit.

★ Memorize all four solos on pages 40 and 41.

145. HUNTERS' CHORUS

Weber

146. DEVIL'S DREAM

Fiddle Tune

ENSEMBLE

147. MARCH GRANDIOSO

Frost

148. FINGER PATTERNS

THEORY
GAME

Fill in the diagrams for the following keys.
Use the letter name of each note and, if needed, the accidental (♭ or ♯).

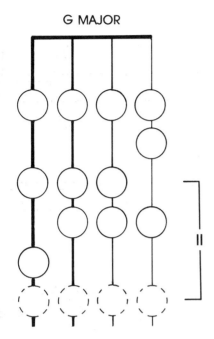

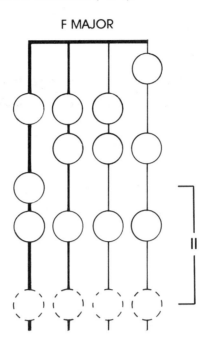

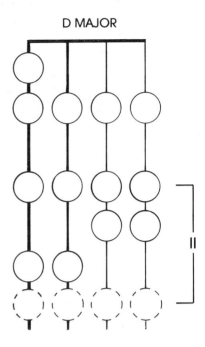

149. WORD SEARCH PUZZLE

THEORY
GAME

```
V R E O R T U F F I W B O F L V Q K D F
V V K D S A J F R O R T Z B C I S A A A
A E B O A H A L O B A R G I I O Y S P K
A H V U S T A T G C O H T I G L M V Z F
H U Z B S W Z R I T P A E S H A M D U V
B E G L S R A Z P N M L F R S O N Y A E
F T X E L I Z T O O A E Q B T S L N M Z
X U S S K I X I R C L T C A B G Q A V A
S D I T P Y T H S C Y R R D O Q S M A N
W E O O D I C H A U K B H K W M G I X Y
S C O P S T E M P O I D B Y L L N C M Q
D Z N O A Z S C S V M U P A T Z B S M L
V L P X R D O L H T S E R F S H Y I O R
Z B Q A P T Y V S M A T T R E S M L O I
A E N D E F L A T A C C E N T R L T Q T
L Y S D G B W T R X W U C G E E M I W A
M Q L B G J J R I A R C O A C Y M A M R
G F J A I V U P N B W U Z A T S I A T D
W E B U O L N Y G V I O L I N O M F V A
J S O N S V L S S N O T E S T P W Y I O
```

30 musical words are hidden in the above puzzle. Can you find them? Be sure to look horizontally, vertically and diagonally and then circle each word that you find.

Below is a list of the 30 words included in the puzzle. Put a check in front of each one as you find it.

ACCENT	CELLO	DYNAMICS	NOTES	SCALE	STRINGS
ARCO	CHROMATIC	ETUDE	PIZZICATO	SHARP	TEMPO
ARPEGGIO	CLEF	FERMATA	POSITION	SLUR	VIBRATO
BASS	DOUBLESTOP	FLAT	RHYTHM	STACCATO	VIOLA
BOW	DUET	FROG	RITARD	STAFF	VIOLIN

MAJOR SCALES

C MAJOR

G MAJOR

D MAJOR

A MAJOR

F MAJOR

B♭ MAJOR

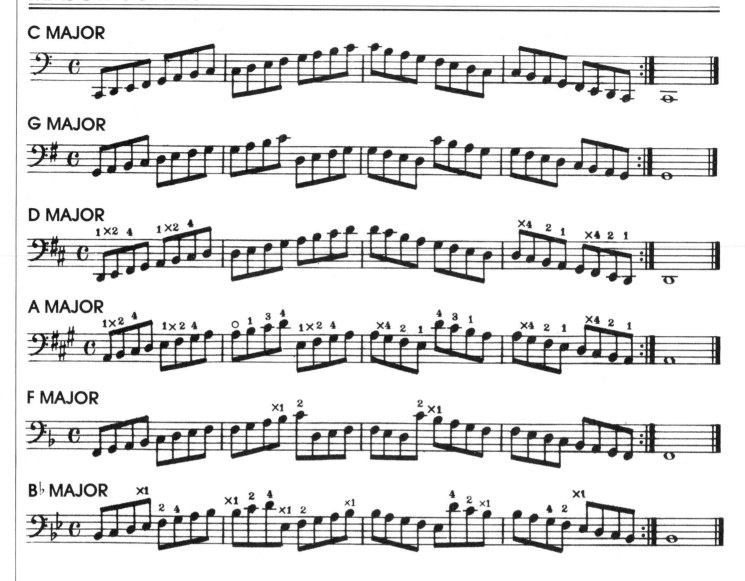

MINOR SCALES (Melodic)

a minor

e minor

b minor

d minor

g minor

CHROMATIC SCALE

BOWINGS

Some of the following bowings may be played in two ways:
   a. Entire pattern on the same pitch of the scale.
   b. Each note on different pitches of the scale.
Your teacher will assign the style of bowing and bow division you are to play.

Bow Divisions

Whole Bow = **W. B.**   Upper Half = **U. H.**   Lower Half = **L. H.**   Middle = **M.**

Slurs

1.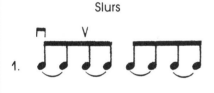

2.

Combination of Slurs and Separate Bows

3.

4.

5.

6.

7.

Slurred Staccato

8.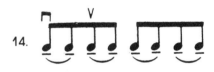

9.

Combination of Slurred Staccato and Slurs

10.

11.

12.

Staccato

13.

Louré

14.

15.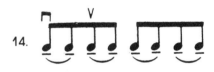

Combination of Slurs and Louré

16.

17.

Triplet

18.  20.

19.  21.

VIBRATO

STRONG and RELAXED are the keywords to developing vibrato. A string player must possess strength so that he/she can play effortlessly and relaxed. The exercises on these three pages are designed to develop both the necessary finger strength and correct vibrato motion of the left hand (arm).

R E L A X

your

S H O U L D E R — A R M — W R I S T — T H U M B — F I N G E R S

throughout

RULES FOR PRACTICING VIBRATO

1. Practice only a few exercises at a time. Stop when your hand, wrist, arm or shoulder becomes tired or tight. Keep all muscles relaxed.
2. A correct slow relaxed motion is always preferred over a tight fast motion.
3. Once vibrato is introduced, it should be practiced each day.

EXERCISES TO DEVELOP FINGER STRENGTH

I. TRILL MOTION

- The finger used for the grace note should spring up quickly. Focus on lifting this finger from the base knuckle as quickly as possible.
- Do more repetitions with your weaker fingers.
- Practice these exercises on all strings.

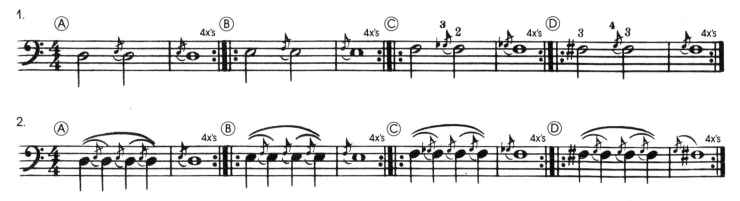

II. LEFT HAND PIZZICATO

- Place only the finger shown on the string — Pluck with a finger motion pulling the string to the side — do not use any wrist motion.
- Work for a good firm, loud and clear pizzicato tone.
- After the pizzicato, the plucking finger should come to rest against the next higher string.
- In Exercise 3 the open D string will sound.
- Practice these exercises on all strings.

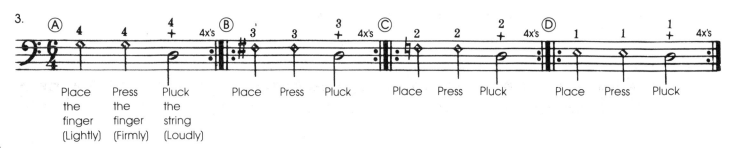

4

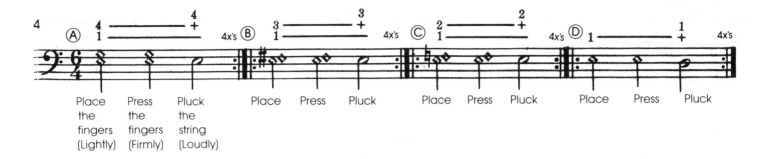

Place the fingers (Lightly) Press the fingers (Firmly) Pluck the string (Loudly)   Place Press Pluck   Place Press Pluck   Place Press Pluck

III. FINGER SLIDES

- These finger slides are good warm-up exercises.
- Keep the finger(s) below the sliding finger down in one location.
- Keep the thumb in one location.
- Use a finger motion only. Move the sliding finger from a curved position to a straight position and back to a curved position.
- Practice these exercises on all strings.

5.

6.

7.

IV. FINGER DISPLACEMENT

- Do this exercise slowly.
- Keep your thumb in the same place throughout this exercise.
- Practice these exercises on all strings.

8.

EXERCISES TO DEVELOP THE CORRECT VIBRATO MOTION

I. **MATCH BOX SHAKE**
    1. Tape a match box shut (with matches inside). Without your instrument, hold your left hand in playing position with the match bow between your thumb and 1st and 2nd fingers.
    2. Shake the match box up and down. This is the motion for vibrato.

II. **POLISHING THE STRING**
    With your instrument in playing position try exercises 1 and 2 in two ways:
    • Without a bow.
    • With a bow.
    1. Put your 2nd finger lightly on the D string. Move your hand and thumb back and forth with your 2nd finger sliding on the string as if polishing the string. See diagram 1. The motion should be like shaking the box of matches. Use a piece of tissue between your sliding finger and the string to help the finger slide back and forth. Use the rhythms listed.

     = move forward    = move backward

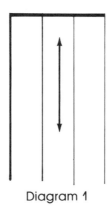

Diagram 1

    2. Practice exercise 1 with your thumb held in one place (regular playing position) against the neck. See diagram 2.
    3. Do exercises 1 & 2 in regular playing position with the bow (without the tissue and the finger firmly on the string).

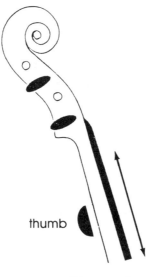

thumb

Diagram 2

RHYTHMS